A Craving for the Goatman

ISBN: 1-930648-44-8

Library of Congress Control Number: 2002110871

Drawings of the Goatman
by David Laughlin, Tucson, Arizona

Type in this book is set in Adobe Garamond
Typography by Karen Nulf, Athens, Ohio

Published by
Deborah J. Benner
GOOSE RIVER PRESS
3400 Friendship Road
Waldoboro, ME 04572-6337

(207)832-6665 Telephone
(775)244-8371 Fax
dbenner@prexar.com

A Craving for the Goatman

POEMS BY ELIZABETH HOBBS

GOOSE RIVER PRESS
Waldoboro, Maine

Foreword

The poems of *A Craving for the Goatman* are not in chrono-logical order, nor are they grouped by subject or location. They are arranged with the hope of surprising the reader with each new selection. The poems were written over a period of roughly twenty years, some on the East Coast, some on the West.

The Goatman refers to Pan, the mythological figure who lured one and all with his music into the delights and dangers of the wild woods. My own Goatman is a collective of the various artists I have known in music, theatre, writing, dance, and the visual arts. They have led me into the wild woods of my imagination, daring me to explore.

Acknowledgments

For their critical judgments and consistent support:

Robert Gringle, Georgann Eubanks, Jane Kendall Mollman, Victoria and Robert George, Pat Hurshell, Nancy Palter, Connie Cross, Babs Murdock, Estelle Watson Sanders,

and Roy Fluhrer, who has never forgotten the "Goatman."

For Bob,
who from the very beginning
has always "dared me to explore"

Section One

Section Two

Section Three

A Craving
for the Goatman

Section One

The Double Helix of DNA
(for Watson, Crick, *et al.*)

We must turn things upside down —
ourselves, our thought, the models that we mold.
The right side up must meet the upside down
to make a match.
The differences are hardly that
but placement makes it so:
one spiral pulsing dark, the other light,
together springing
      into life.

Effort, error, wild love, stubborn thought,
the miner's courage — blend to foil the Sphinx
until at last we see
and do not have to pay the ancient price.

Spiraling forms wrapped round each other —
it is impossible to gaze upon their coil
without the gasp of pleasure.

Farewell to Delphi

I have invented the passion between us.
You do not long as I do
for the throat-deep kiss,
the mouth that searches,
the thrust that warms.
Your pleasures lie inward,
mind transported, flesh forgotten.

I have invented. I have put on
reflecting prism glasses,
my bits and pieces of wine goblets,
dew and ocean mist.
I have mistook your morning greeting.
You cannot fulfill my prophecy.

Goat-foot Man

And still I crave you, goat-foot man,
though you have led me in the frantic chase
with pipes that promise but never name their price.
I do not want to play your savage tune,
my hidden melody is secret-sweet.
But willingly I tear my feet
and rend the ordered fabric that I wear:
each day you force me to create
that varied music that I hear.

Lesson from Sparta

The fur is soft, delicious to the touch.
Who could resist holding it close,
this little fox of love
breathing next to my heart.

But o, the price
when the fox bites.

This Poem Is Not about the Ancient Greeks

My name is Cassandra
and I cannot save you.
I can see the knives flashing,
the bathwater bloodied red,
but you will not hear my cry.
You will stride through the lion gate
full of your lusty manhood,
ready to bed your killer.

And I, because you have wanted me,
I too must die.

Oh God, You're Gone Again.

Every feature of the landscape
is much the same—and yet—
    if I could understand magnetics,
    the power of light waves,
I could explain just how
    with you the landscape changes shape,
    shimmers in your force field.

My skin knows but cannot tell
how as you leave, the earth cools
and the bleak strangeness sets in.

I'm never ready.

Mock-Union

How is it that you place your head?
And why should I care?
How is it that I should lie
where you have lain,
molding my body to your bed
as tight as if it were you?

Bodies do not remain behind,
their three dimensions stay three.
They are not bas-reliefs
with which to decorate
a wall of longing.

When we are gone,
all beds are as blank of us
as though we had never been.

So why do I believe
that in this bed you cover me,
that while I lie here
we are joined again?

MR. WEATHERMAN, A BIT OF TROUBLE, IF YOU PLEASE

Where is the thunder you promised for today?
God knows I didn't want a storm to smash the world,
no knocked-down poles, dead bodies, and sizzling wires;
but I could have used some fireworks,
some of your real action, some jazzy entertainment,
some recompense for this mild wet incessance.

So why don't you have some fun,
bring on your cymbals, do your bellydance in the sky?
Come on, roll your pins at me,
then let me breathe the clearing air,
and hunt the rainbow's end.

Spring for Solace

They are not enough,
though they are lovely,
the tulips, crocus, hyacinth,
the new leaves of the bleeding heart.
For them, I have spent my penny for the soul.

But the soul wants steady warmth,
not brilliant color,
the savor of another soul
that does not fade with summer.

For Tobias Wolff
(after reading *This Boy's Life*)

My feet are sucking up mud
the way yours did in the field
when you and your buddies stole the gas,
but the mud is in my mind,
in dreams – the kind where
you try to run upstairs but seem
to have forgotten your oxygen tank
or else someone else forgot
to finish off the stairs or made
the passageway so cramped
you'd have to bend over double
to get out, or hardly breathe,
like the feeling you get in the spiral
staircase in the *House of Seven Gables*.

I never did steal gas, but I guess
I would if I had to. You have
to have gas to get away.

The Men Who Make Love

The men who make love are clean.
Their beds are smooth and fragrant,
their mouths sweet with promise.

Their each day's sweat is new
and unfamiliar, quick to run away
in each ritual cleansing of the night.

Their hair floats softly,
free of custom,
curls fresh and damp
as early crocus in the sun.

These men make love, stay clean,
and bear no fruit but beauty.

I Remember You Best

in dim light
with your dark head
bent over my breast,
the white mound of my flesh
made live and warm
by the strength
of your mouth.

I wish a Rembrandt could have painted you so.

For Paul at Two

I hold you close,
your body shivering from play
in the cold outdoor pool.

I stroke your red-gold curls,
remembering my mother's hair—
your great-grandmother.
I look into your blue, blue eyes
and see her there,
that direct blood line
drawn so clear.

Latest Visit to a Friend

In your house
there are differences
in seventy days—
daisies in a coffee jar,
(I like the daisies)
sheet music on the window shelf.
(She plays the flute, you say)
She has left a cape I would have chosen
and boots that I would wear;
she is a presence visible,
but a presence so far kept contained.

I feel and fear her fear and hunger,
and I cannot find the cup
I used to drink from.

Yellow Leaves

This year
the yellow leaves refuse to fall,
though it is past their prime,
and we are glad.

We need their color
in the crisping air.
Their movement warms the sight,
they mellow fall
and hold the winter back.

We know too well
that after nights of rushing wind,
we will awake to find again
the brittle time
when rhododendrons –
grayish-green –
hunch in their leaves
so narrow
we might almost reach for them,
like housewives snapping beans.

Testament to My Child

I have heard you cry deep and hard
for friends, for pets, for lost loves.
I will never hear you cry for me.

I do not believe, of course,
that either you or I will die.
I cannot imagine being a memory
that you discuss with others,
my eccentric image
no longer in my control.

I rather expect
to be an eternal Huckleberry Finn,
eavesdropping on grief,
slightly ashamed of my tricks,
and ready to return.

STARDUST

I read the other day
that we are all stardust,
made of stardust,
and I believe it.
Especially you –
you left this house
for only two weeks,
but the house knew.
The brilliance went out of it.
The charged ions
returned to stable state.
Nothing crackled, and the air
was no longer spun with magic.

Moonshot

They have taken the moon from us.
Closer, it moves farther away.
The faces of love are gone,
replaced by known and sterile craters,
strewn with the hardware of our pride.
Men have stopped their solitary midnight worship,
idolatrous now of charts and dials.

But distance still is all,
and Diana will take vengeance.
She cannot with safety be possessed,
marked and measured.

Short-lived the lust
that hunts the huntress.
Her chastity violated,
she strides the heavens
with a venomed quiver,
waiting out the cycles,
playing with her prey,
coolly always coolly,
ready with her own apocalypse
when our antic revels
are ended.

THE NICEST CHEMISTRY LESSON

Your molecular structure
must be attuned to mine.
There are lots of things
I can touch – even people –
and nothing happens.

Not so with you.
Your hands on me,
your breath on my neck,
and all my atoms run amok,
beating one another
in delicious frenzy.

Give Me Lilacs

Give me lilacs while I live,
no guilty lilies after.

Lilacs are brief
and speak to me
of lost wind and sun and rain,
of shaggy, faroff doorways.

So seldom, so welcome,
lilacs each time give strength;
my harsh New England
waits for them to bloom again.

The Rule of Law

We have agreed upon
a system of private spheres
which will roll smoothly
touching only at single points
able to run clockwise
or counter—
but always
tangentially.

Separate we roll
toward the ten pins
and the end
of the long slick lane.

BRIEF SHELTER

On a day of finest weather
they built a fragile summer house,
furnished it with gleeful reeds
and dry rushes of warmth.
They worked with silky eyelids
shuttered to half-light.
And then they lay,
while over each other they drew
cool veils of illusion.

A summer's day is long and mild
and casts its shadows late
into memory where summer lives
when houses built of finest weather
do not last.

As I Mourn Men

How many dead,
too soon returned
to earth, to air,

while I still see
and hear and dance
without their arms about me
or their mouths hot on mine.

Must it be the fate of women
to live in memory,
racked with loss after loss,
warmed but unsatisfied
by the breathy goodnight kiss
of children, however dear?

Flesh never learns to say goodbye.

Concubine

He will be back
and you will be there
waiting.

He will believe he wants you
and you will know
the difference
between desire
and fear of no desire.

But you will wait
like the cool observer
you have learned to be.

You will mouth the little words,
and reassure, and stroke,
and watch it happen.

You will lie open to him,
willing liquid to come.

You will flex trained muscles
to lock his body into passion.

He will believe. He will be back.

PERSPECTIVE

The azaleas have splashed red
against the grey wall.
I almost objected,
trained as I am by decades of protest,
seeing the red at a distance,
thinking it spray paint –
as violent as blood.

I am twice caught:
both by my first dark vision of beauty
and then by the puzzle.

Red is red after all.

A Tour of Tao House
(Home of Eugene O'Neill and his third wife, Carlotta Monterey)

There was a room we didn't see.
The guide misjudged her pace,
or so she said.

There was a room that no one ever saw,
as private as the mind that lived there.

This was a house of coldness and color,
of tiled floors and stark white basalt walls
and ceilings of vaulted blue
crafted to trick the eye,
like the green mirror in the hall
that made ghosts of us all,
like the roof tiles painted black
where we expected red.

And everywhere Carlotta's gliding shape,
the caretaking woman taking care
that no one else could take care.

I see her nails as scarlet,
carmine-tipped, ripping open
letters that he would never read,

closing doors that lay between them
sealing them apart,
door by lacquered door

while he hunched in his airy cage
turned toward Mount Diablo
writing in a hand that shrank
like angels dancing on the heads of pins.

I see her soul as lacquered,
hard and slick,
her nails longer, sharper,

her eyes made crystalline
by whatever she saw
in that private room
we were not allowed to see.

Summer Flowers

Nasturtiums with pansy faces
flood the air with fragrance.
In the darkness of our shaded room,
they blaze of love. No one sells them,
they have to be given. When I leave,
I will not press them in a book
anymore than I would press you.
They have to live, to wilt, to die,
impossible to keep, impossible to forget—

Visit to Your Grave

My nails are caked
with dirt I clawed up
from the flat granite.
The sod was closing in,
grown tight and thick
until I could hardly read
your name.

I've never been one
for ritual visits or ceremonial stones.
I expected nothing. I had no tools.

Yet in an instant I was frantic,
scrabbling as though someone were drowning,
as though a mine had caved in
and I had to rescue you
with my bare hands.

ROMANTICS

You are not my prince,
my lord, my king,
nor I your consort.
We do not live in castles;
ours is the stuff of everyday.

We do the Sunday puzzles,
tramp across town,
hurt one another
in unexpected ways.

Aliens in each other's worlds,
we delight in these visits,
these forays into new unknowns.

Section Two

Discovering You, Grandfather, in New Hampshire
(For William Byron Hobbs 1881-1958)

We drove higher and higher
up the dirt road you traveled daily
during years we could not find you.

We tried to imagine
what lay ahead where
horses had regularly labored
to reach the Stagecoach Inn.

The inn is gone, the inn
you made into your recluse home.
But we met your nearest neighbor,
whose fear of you and your guns
turned into gingersnaps and tea,
into shared love of horses, dogs,
cats, raccoons, and all manner
of living things.

We were shown pictures of you
bare-chested – playing with kittens,
treating your housekeeper's child,
her grandchildren, far better
than you had your own.

We are deep into the mystery
of your life, your fabled cruelties,
your love of nature and of solitude,
your lonely death in the house
on the abandoned road to Groton.

And we, who never met you,
stand by your grave and debate
ethics. Should my husband,
your grandson, order a replacement
stone with a handsome design?
Would he then be giving you
undue honor, you who disowned
seven children and beat a wife
into madness?

Scoring the Orange

Somewhere I learned how
to cut off the ends
sparingly
so as not to damage the fruit.
Somewhere I learned to score
the peel – not too deeply.
Somewhere I learned to eat
the slices.

Yet I can't remember
who I watched.
I remember only the halves
my father pressed down
on the squeezer to make
thick pulpy juice we prized
in those dark 30's days.

We were so fortunate, my mother said.

Voyage

I have been dealing with Death
the best way I can

last night for once
the ship did not sail
without me

I even had my passport
my tickets

yet the sailing was not sweet
drenched with the sea
drenched with my own sweat
I ran from deck to deck
frantic with loss
unprepared for holiday
so costly, so hard won

you were with me, telling me
with all the kindness
you could muster
that nothing else was needed –
I was there

On Keeping an Old Cup

I can't remember this tendency to rust.
We drank cold milk out of tin cups
on Memorial Day. Always we parked
on the wooded river bluff at the edge
of the Yarmouth cemetery, visiting
all the relatives we had never known
and one we had, one who had visited
with us.

A luxuriant place, shady and fragrant,
old stones making the past real—
Grandfather Eldridge honored
by the Grand Army of the Republic,
every year a little flag—
one of the Winslow boys, aged 19
and "lost at sea," surrounded
by the many Winslow babies
who had not lived a year.

But that was after the roast beef and lettuce
between thick slices of the bread Mother had made
and slabs of her spice cake, no frosting.

The bandstand thumped with patriotism.
We sang from the heart all the words we knew.
Maybe there were speeches; I doubt I ever listened.

Mostly I remember the wide tin cups
that held the cold on a hot day.

Oysterwoman

Everyone tells me it's not worth it
trying to pry pearls from an oyster,
hard to open it yet leave it
intact for later pearls,
easier if you just want to kill it,
but even so, hard.

The pearl means nothing to the oyster,
a sandy irritation only.
Yet it won't give a pearl away
until I get my tools and heavy gloves
and become again a shucker
determined to find the warm translucence
I know is there,
until I don again my ocean boots
against water and wild winds.

I have no feeling for the oyster.
I just want his pearls.

Tearing Apart a Life

Take down the pictures,
fill in the holes.
Empty the cupboards,
scrub the floors.

Fold the blankets,
forget those they covered,
forget the rain,
the softness of snow,
the delicate tracing of fingers,
the words, the whispers.

Eat ice cream at midnight,
forget, forget all you know.

MOTHER 1889-1989

Only now am I getting to know you,
only now have you told me the stories
I needed a long time ago,
and even now I'm sure there's more
of what you really were.

I never knew the others
called you Good Eldridge
as you marched the 3rd grade boys
around the school basement on rainy days,
to the snap and rhythm of your words,
upbeat, upbeat all the way.

You say you never worried about me.
That I can't believe. I was plenty
to worry about, with my long hair
and my troubled heart.

I won't forget the safe stories
of sleeping, three weeks old,
in a hotel bureau drawer in Boston,
or the train trips in California at two
with your wicker rocking chair
held high over your papa's head
as he strode the aisles from car to car.

You've always known more
than you would say. Tell it now,
I need it before you go.

LETTER TO MY FATHER
AFTER A TALK WITH MY BROTHER

How many years did you love the lilacs
and I never knew? You had no sense of smell,
how could I have known you shared my lust?
You never spoke of it to me,
or so my memory tells me.
I should have known from the dresses
that we wore, Mother clothing us
in pale lavender, sisters paired –
and Mother lived to please you.

How I wish you could have known
the fragrance that I wait for –
April lilacs in the West,
June on the New England shore.

O Father, gone these many years,
what other passions did we share,
never spoken of, never dared?

ANGST

The circuits
of your brain
throb like
subway trains
hurtling
through a
New York night
express trains
hardly stopping
rattling, pounding
swaying to some
computer programmed
long ago.

All the conductors
have been shot
or just
walked off
the job.

CORRESPONDENCE

I sat here in the middle of December
bringing you up to date
on moves and houses, trips to Tucson,
plans to see the opera in New York City.

It was the longest Christmas card
I ever wrote you, even had a poem enclosed
about my cold attic room in Maine
when I was a kid.

This year I was pleased that I had mailed it
early enough to reach you before the 25th,
not Valentine's Day or the 4th of July,
as is my wont.

And all that time you were lying
seven months dead – somewhere –
buried by a brother
I didn't even know you had.

Today, I opened the card
the post office had "returned to sender,
forwarding order expired."

There were my cheery final words to you:
"And what's your news, darlin'?"

On Contemplating Necessary Separations

I do not want to sleep alone.
I have some memory of the tribe
wrapped in furs,
breathing in quiet patterns of repose,
warm back against full belly
in the deep night shifting,
covered by the human quilt of comfort
that strengthens the blood
against the Arctic ice.

En Route to Portland, Oregon
after Mt. St. Helens

The world seems normal enough:
Greyhound station-bustle, bad coffee, farewell tears;
and on the road the green world,
the astonishingly crafted yet always accepted
green highway world,
leading to a city that does not believe,
cannot fathom (dare not?)
that the foliage world
and the Greyhound air-conditioned world
can vanish in a twitch of Gaea's thigh.

37,000 years have made us placid.

And I, in the easeful pleasure
of this scheduled metal, breathing air
filtered, I hope, from silica darts,
I too cannot believe in more than inconvenience,
I cannot believe Pompeii.

I refuse those awesome powers
long trapped in catalogued museums
where people meet for tea.
I want my Greyhound world.
It, too, is awesome but its process
hidden, its miracles of fusion and transformation
ordinaried into bad taste and neon green.
I refuse this new Atlantis of dun and pumice
where old gods strut, new-defiant to be seen.

Hey, Cobra, I'm Coming to See You.

I haven't had enough yet
of your shiny undulations.
I want to see how good I am —
after you get me mesmerized —
at dodging that sharp red tongue
you dart out every now and then.

Brief Gentle Neighbor
(after the Rape)

It is not possible to tell what lies
behind your covered windows,
some of you perhaps still there
hidden behind the ragged blue shade
I gave you, diffidently, to keep you safe
from all the tiger eyes I feared
would devour you, one way or another.

Have you moved?

Before you pounded on my door that morning
quivering, barefoot, naked beneath your thin jacket,
violated beyond recall, I had feared for you.
Something about your eyes moved too fast,
your shoulders carried too high as though shivering,
some animal velvet about you always.

The wreath you made is still in the window.
Have you left it there, unable to touch its irony,
the bitter hour you spent with the stranger,
the wreath staring at you helpless
that used to cheer you toward Christmas?

Thoughts in a Roadside Park

I had never expected
to forget names,
surely not yours.
Can I have loved you
only with my mouth,
my hands, the nerve ends
you controlled?
I had thought to keep you
somewhere safe and sacred,
I assume, cannot recall.
I have replaced you now
too often. You are mingled,
muted, cold too long.

The daisies here are real,
the sun, the fragrance.
But you, my dear, are gone.

As If

It is as if, you said, there were a beast snarling – ready,
but not yet willing – to pounce.

As if there were a trap covered with branches and damp moss,
eager to engulf you if you took one wrong step.

You live on the brink of disaster, you say, grateful for delay,
but always edgy, always waiting for the tearing of your throat
by Churchill's black dog.

(Note: Winston Churchill referred to his recurrent depression as
his "black dog.")

I Am Forever the Woman

bearing food and drink
even into the wilderness.
And you will always be the man,
forcing fire from earth.
Were you to die, I could not leave off
my planning for you in your eternal tomb.
Were I to go, you would still bring branches
to warm my cooling bones.

DIRECTIONS

There used to be little question,
graves were easy to locate:
family plot or town burying ground.

But today you had to call me
on your cell phone to ask
directions to the new-dug grave
of a friend you'd known well
for twenty years.

And I in turn had to scramble
through phone books,
calling this office and that
until I got the right person
who could help me help you
get there in time for the burial.

We sounded so business-like,
even cheerful, that it took a minute
for the shudder to hit me –
the thought that one day,
one day, one of us will have to deal
with the loss of the other.

And next, of course,
the chilling selfish question –
which of us will bring
the flowers?

PHYSICS, DECEMBER 26, 1981

As Hitler marched, Warsaw radio
defiantly played Chopin
over and over again Chopin's *Polonaise*
Paderewski playing Chopin
Hitler playing war
the world listening

And when abruptly the music stopped
when Chopin finally was silenced
Poland had been devoured

Today we searched the grocery shelves
for the last jar of Krakow black-currant jam
feeling obscene that we could reduce
such suffering to regret that there will be
no shipments of our breakfast jam
from Poland

Tomorrow over lunch, German bankers
will debate losses, of assets perhaps, or lives
and Sunday, David Brinkley
with new strategies for old politics
In Canada next week, how many seekers of asylum
as all the while the gassings, the manglings
into a new unspeakable Solidarity

And so for Poland
we will hang our helpless scarlet ribbons
and we will watch the nightly news
and somewhere, somehow, the airways
still will hold the sound of Paderewski
playing Chopin's brilliant *Polanaise*.

I KINDA WISH I WERE HOPPING A TRAIN,

a train from the old days,
full of crystal and heavy silverware,
fresh flowers on every table.

At night I'd lie pristine in my narrow bunk
rushing toward you in the sweet dark
or else I'd smuggle you aboard
to giggle with me through the hours
emerging sedate,
responding to the last call for breakfast.

BOTANY IN THE RAIN FOREST

First, the nurse tree must die.
It must fall,
no matter slow or fast,
it must let go of sky,
lie forever lengthwise
in deadly moist embrace.
It must rot,
beautifully, pungently,
opening pores to seed.

Its straightline nurselings
will confound the innocent:
"What planted such a row
in these chaotic woodlands?"
There will be no trace.

After the final consummation,
the line of new trees will remain.

But first, and long before, the nurse must die.

BAPTISM

They named you Ophelia, a lovely liquid name,
though they didn't know what it meant.
And when your hair was long enough to float,
they found a tall thin man of God
to hold you under the waters of a muddy stream
until you knew that sin was not to be trifled with
but sanctity made the chest ache and the breath come hard.

Ophelia, sent harshly into the universal nunnery,
expand your lungs, braid up your streaming hair.
Swim harder away.

THE SISTERHOOD

He being gone,
she is the newest member,
dry-eyed, seeming to smile,
(prepared by ritual)
relieved. Frightened
by new silences, new spaces.

They know as the uninitiated
cannot know. They gather
round her.

She asks to be alone,
needing to worry the gap in her life
as though it were a missing
tooth.

ALL OF US SEEM TO HAVE ONE,

a cellar of the mind
where things are waiting
like mice squealing in corners
or pipes leaking onto books
that we had stored.

The underbelly of our lives,
floored in grit and concrete
that you taste when you fall hard
down stairs that betray you,
where you lie grateful
that you can still add 2 and 2
while the red lump blooms
on the head you smashed.

You want to make magic private rooms,
hideaways in the warm dark,
but there is no money for renovation
and the only magic leaves you troubled
when your uncle's fingers find what
you had not truly known was there,
and you run upstairs to daylight to denounce
the too-soon pleasure of your seven years.

THE LONG YEAR

The year has been ruled
by a kind of Malthusian theory.
Malthus had it all muddled of course –
he should have played around with time.

If he had loved someone like you,
he would have realized that ordinary days
march along one plus one
but days away from you multiply
and flex themselves into crazy geometrics,
self-contained circles, cubes of lonesomeness,
and pyramids of longing that pierce the heart.

RESPONSE TO ARIEL DORFMAN OF CHILE
READING FOR AMNESTY INTERNATIONAL
AT THE DUKE MUSEUM OF ART

Behind you a white wall, very clean
Beside you twenty white chairs, empty
empty white metal chairs
clean metal cold and perfect

Who should be in them, who is missing?

You speak of vile matters
speak in blacks and reds
You make our safe stomachs lurch
You bind our safe heads with fillets of madness

I believe you
And I fear them

the 'they' who are always coming
to get me, to get you, to get all of us
the 'they' who are never far enough from us
the 'they' who are among us and in us—

Reluctance

Two thousand years ago
I wanted to be earth,
but there was some question:
my earth around your sun,
your sun around my earth.

Now after Galileo, I must see
that I am one of many earths,
that I must circle your sun,
that I must acknowledge
extraordinary celestial pull,
the fearsome pull of earth's waters.
And I must see the falling bodies,
those frequent falling bodies;
I must know that I may fall
out of this orbit.

SUMMER CONFERENCE

At the lectern, the feet wear
bright red hightops, the bodies
suspenders and shorts and tee shirts.

On them, it all looks funky, looks good,
this confederacy of poets trailing
acolytes who laugh too soon, too much,

prophets from another country
who have done us the favor
of living hard and telling us about it—
the come that didn't come,
all-night retching, hospital stays,
doubts that claw in grey light.

Such cheerful faces read aloud
their litany of disaster
and after the reading laugh
as they sign up for beer
and a beach party.

MATER NON DOLOROSA

That child you suckled
and held close to your heart,
stroked and petted
like the flower all babies are,
you now believe has earned
his place in Paradise –
and yours as well.

You rejoice that his young body
has not flinched from unspeakable pain,
that he has held his finger steady
on the detonator that will shred him
into the tiniest of pieces.

Tess Gallagher Reads Ray Carver
at Elliott Bay Books

Someone thought to place on the reading stand
two red tulips in a single vase.
Tess is talking about late bloomers,
flipping her long hair back
and pronouncing the title "Car"
in the Washington-state way, hard,
far from Boston but with an Irish lilt all the same.

She stands on the same spot
where both of them stood hardly a year ago,
and I think, "At least now it has happened
and therefore can't crush her again"
except, unless, it still crushes her to read
with no antiphonal voice to tease her.

But then she laughs, or they do,
and it's hard to tell who's saying what:
"Don't get weird on me, Babe,
don't get weird."

The voice doesn't falter
and in the Strait of Juan de Fuca,
two lights gleam.

It Was Cold in the Mornings,

your nose told you that.
You had only to touch it to know
how your feet would feel
when they poked out of the warmth
you had stored in the night.

Every evening you took the soapstone
that had been heating all afternoon,
wrapped it in newspaper, then in flannel,
before you started the icy trek
to the third floor, where the only heat
was your own, what you brought.

The sheets were cotton flannel this time of year
and the quilts heavy, comforting.
You wore socks to bed and raced your feet
back and forth to create friction
until the soapstone did its work.

You huddled deep down with a flashlight
to use for just one more chapter
after you were supposed to be asleep,
your breath moist under the covers.

And now a continent away,
you open your windows at night
to bring in December's delicious ice.

MID-JANUARY AT SEVEN A.M.

The rain has stopped.
It is almost light enough
to dare the streets.

The daily news lies on the lawn.
No ice, only sodden paths
lead to its treasures, its shocks,
its clashes of opinion.

Outside the air is damp and good to breathe.
I want to hold the promise of this day
while the neighborhood sleeps.

Every early waking is my gift—
unwrapped too fast, used up too soon.

Section Three

Punky Is Probably Immortal

I have you all mixed up
with the third grade
and Miss Shaw
and hot wet injustice.

You called me Lizzie, cackling
and pointing at the pee puddle
I had made when Miss Shaw
wouldn't let us leave until
we had finished all our math.

Miss Shaw was like that.
Once she kept me after,
until five o'clock, to find
a math mistake I hadn't even made.

Third grade is like that.
The boys get mean,
and the teachers get worried
about skills tests
and god knows what.
No more milk and cookies,
it's time
to stay within the lines.

And Punky is always there,
in some form or other,
no matter what grade
you get to, no matter
how far you travel
from that snowy schoolyard.

I never knew what happened
to Miss Shaw, but I've heard rumors
about you, Punky, and just as mean
as you, I hope they're true.

Approaching Your Birth

It was supposed to happen November 4
so I got an absentee ballot. Couldn't
let Goldwater win. Your father was rehearsing
a show, down in the Village. Before long,
you would go to rehearsals with him
and put in your own two cents' worth.

But right now you were getting ready to breathe,
enjoying your last few swims
in the warm amniotic fluid I couldn't even feel.

I was scared, of course, remembering the vicious
contractions that every month had brought me
for more than twenty years. This could be worse,
they all told me. How, O God, how?

Worse, too, than the night terrors?
Imagining you eyeless, deaf, brain-damaged
from my first trimester when German measles
stalked my classroom, and no one in Portland, Maine,
had records of my immunity or lack of it.

Worse than the guilt that ignorance brings,
the number of times in my 7th, 8th, 9th months
when I urged your father to drive into me
until I rocked with orgasm more powerful
than the fear of harming you?

That October was warm in Manhattan,
the drive across Central Park like a Leaf-Peepers tour
of New England, all tawny and golden,
rich with leaf mold and the promise of harvest.

At Flower-Fifth Avenue Hospital, they took me away alone,
clutching my two *New Yorkers* to see me through.
Your father, banished by medical authority,
caught the subway downtown to rehearsal.

And you kept pushing your dark witch's head
through an opening I could only imagine
from the dry drawings of Biology class.

The doctor said later that I wrenched the IV from my arm,
causing the nurses all manner of trouble
just because I wanted to turn over
and was too drugged to say so.

All I know is that at first there was a searing pain,
then disbelief four hours later
to find "Hobbs female" on my plastic bracelet.

At six a.m. you and I looked at each other
for the first time straight on
and have not stopped looking since.

CENTRAL DISTRICT, SEATTLE

There is nothing innocent here
where day and night
the red and blue flash past
encircling us.

We wake sometimes (often)
to hear the little pops
that could be cars,
more likely deaths
or threats at least,
pop pop pop pop–POP

From the depths of sleep
we wake our fingers
to dial the amulet 911,
911, 911 with a marvelous ease
automatic
and we never know
who bled while we slept
the rest of our night away.

Rosario Beach

The smell of summer is back,
an attar of cedars, balsam,
and invisible hyacinths.
Sweat is back
and the need for cool water.
The paths and knolls of parks
are full of lovers,
and you lie on moss
sighing content
and asking
for three more strawberries.

So Few Trees

So few trees on Waterville Street,
not enough beauty, never enough.
Trees would have helped.
I remember lying on the stiff wool
of the parlor rug in underpants,
my face turned toward the ocean
hot blocks away, trying to sleep.

I remember mostly how my bare skin itched
and there were no trees to shade us in the house
which hardly cooled in the July night.

There must have been trees somewhere on that street.
I scuffed through golden leaves in autumn
and smelled their pungency,
and somewhere there was a tree the big boys hid behind
who made me scared and glad I was a girl.

CAMELS

You have torn out
all the holly bushes.
What will you feed the camels
when they come to call?

They bite, you know.

Zoological Instruction

The same snake that coils around a creature
to crush it is not the one that sinks its fangs
into living flesh, is not the one that glides
into a forbidden spot expanding and poisoning
from within.

But they are all snakes and they all kill.

I am no handler of snakes. Take your writhings
to a temple of holy believers.

LETTER

I left you at seven this morning
in the parking lot of the bakery,
a warm wind from the ocean
and the darkness as companions.

I drove up Highway 26
with the smell of your whisky
and tobacco permeating
my car, my clothes.
And then I heard
that Hugo had died –
at the height, they said.

I never got to argue with him
as I do with you
about the nature of pain
and the pleasure
some poets get from it.

But I would probably have failed
with him as I do with you.
I could only have watched him
let his vision extract
its last bitter price.

I don't even know
what more I want to tell you.

There's no ending to this letter,
no ending to our struggle
to resist each other's vision
even while we keep on wishing
to be seen.

White Woman in a Southern Town

It is getting dark,
nearly five,
nearly December.
I have missed a turn
in this labyrinth of one-way streets
and unmarked directions,
my well-being vanished
in these neighborhoods
that don't want me,
don't trust me.

No one else will hurt me—
I know that—
I myself the only menace,
making wrong turn
after wrong turn,
the bile of panic
in my closing throat.

Only strangers to a town
should plan its markers,
only those who don't know
east from west, north from south.

April, This Year

Once again, there is a last day,
a last time to wind the striking clock,
a last ride in the country,
a last talk.

Once again, nothing is finished,
nothing sorted and filed for good.
Fragments of words hang in air
becoming moist.

In a chilly anteroom in Maine fifty years ago,
my aunts piled Christmas presents
on a black and silver glider
which now sways silent on a Carolina porch,
the seat suspended, like me,
in this Southern spring.

Plea to My Friend, Caught

The hidden strings, hidden strings,
you dare not brush at them.
You twitch, obeying their grip
of gossamer.

O Gulliver, get up. You face
only pin pricks and thread.
The web has long since dried.
The spider's dead.

SMALL-HEART

What does it cost the body to lie clenched,
centered on a tiny gnarl of fear?

The Chinese use two characters for danger,
small and heart, to speak of the heart
that shrinks itself to guard against intrusion,
hardening all its soft loose pulsings,
the flow of blood securely damned.

VISITING GRANDMOTHER

I had to go there on Sunday afternoons.
No one really asked me to,
who was her namesake,
but it felt good to cause such delight,
to feel the warm dry hands sandwich mine –
"It must be Elizabeth,
no one else has hands so small."

She was soft, her face, her hands.
I did not know there was a body
inside those usual black clothes,
or hair beneath the usual black cap.
I was not concerned.

I was there to please myself,
to feel my specialness,
the oldest child of her favorite, Charlie.
I did not know that grandmothers
were said to give you toys
and cookies and laps to sit upon.
I doubt I would have cared.

At least ten years
I visited her in the same place,
where she sat in state in the Morris chair
by the dining room table,
her eyes growing more clouded,
her grip tighter with her 97 years.

How I loved her age. How I loved
my own eternal youth.

One day when I was sixteen,
I rode my bicycle the length
of the Eastern Promenade,
in the wind of an April afternoon.

It was the only year I rode a bike,
the only day I felt so free,
the very day she died.

OLD LOVER

I called you today.
(Did you get my last letter?)
Your line was busy.
(Good sign – at least you're home.)
And then we spoke
and I remembered why I had loved you.

You were eager to tell me
about your latest love –
"This one will last, I think."

I'm glad it will
and glad it isn't me.

You were not meant for my every day,
just a rich *paté* I still crave now and then.

New Place

When we were eight years old, you and I,
and had not met as yet,
someone built this house for us,
planned the long living room full of light,
built windowsills deep for pots of crocus.

Someone slept in the long bedroom,
breathed fast in the passions of the night,
planted dogwood, breathed fast again
in the blooming of the spring.

This was the house each of us had dreamed of,
like none we had ever known,
but only longed for, like a dollhouse
we could never hope to own.

Something deep and primitive
is working in me across this continent,
where I have lived so much alone.
I feel you preparing for us,
as an ancient man might glory
in finding a new and spacious cave to take me to.

What nonsense. I'm the one who found the place.

But it is you who ready it,
who spread the hard-killed furs,
who keep me warm.

LETTER FROM NORTH CAROLINA

Once we went to Venice,
a lifetime ago,
and stayed in a room
on the Grand Canal.
It was hotter than we expected
and dirtier, too,
but it was Venice.

Tonight there's Venice on tv,
shimmering still
though a sad story of decay,
of sinking toward a muddy doom
which even then we knew of.

Tonight we remember the Bridge of Sighs,
the Doges' palaces and dungeons,
that curious mix of opulence
and intrigue, the cynical use of power.

Floods of pigeons rose daily
from St. Mark's Square, soaring startled.

Every afternoon we lay in the sweet sweat
of September, later picked our way seeking
supper past Venetian streets of water,
heads full of what poets and painters
had told us.

O, who can know Venice?

We know the fire that burns here on our hearth
and in the backyard the camellia bush
full of pale pink December blooms.

AMATEURISM

I have rehearsed your absence –
the violent waking from dreams
to find an empty bed.
I practice aloneness
and speak the lines of sorrow.

But my concentration nightly flees
in the warmth of your sweet flesh,
and for that final performance
I am forever unprepared.

Visitors to the Sea Islands
(for Jamie Wyeth)

The islands are not easy,
are folded in on themselves
like budded roses or
pharaohs' treasures
rife with warning
to let those treasures lie.

Each weathered cottage,
each Spartan room, sits
open in the sun and wind,
fresh as a child's eyes
hiding everything that matters.

Somebody in the House

Just to hear
you rattle around,
loading the dishwasher,
running up and down the stairs,
rustling the newspapers —

just to smell your toast,
your coffee brewing,
the hyacinths you bought
in full bloom —

just to see you in your favorite chair,
intent on your book or a tv show,
to watch your face
when I tell you a truth
you can scarcely believe
because it praises you so —

Just this — even if nothing more —
would be enough.

A native of Maine, Elizabeth Hobbs currently divides her
time between Maine and North Carolina. (She is a member
of both the Maine Writers and Publishers Alliance and
the North Carolina Writers' Network.) Her work has appeared
in such publications as *Bittersweet*, *Literary Arts* (Oregonian),
Written Arts (King County Arts Council), *Poetry* (Seattle
Times), *Camellia*, and *Psychopoetica* (Hull, England).
Her poetry cards have sold at various shops, and bookstores
such as Powell's in Portland, Oregon.

Hobbs has taught literature and creative writing in colleges,
as well as in public and independent schools. She has
served as Artist-in-Residence for the Manzanita, Oregon,
Fine Arts Council, for the Creative Arts Program at Camp
Hawthorne, Raymond, Maine, in an ongoing residency,
and for the Fine Arts Center in Greenville, South Carolina.

Elizabeth Hobbs has appeared on television in the Cactus
Poets series and was a frequent reader in the Castalia
series at the University of Washington under Nelson Bentley.
She holds a BA *cum laude* degree from Bates College,
an MA from the University of Washington, and member-
ship in both Actor's Equity and Phi Beta Kappa.